# THE ANATOMY OF
# A BOOK DEAL

# THE ANATOMY OF
# A BOOK DEAL

## JIM STRADER

TINSEL ROAD BOOKS

SANTA MONICA, CALIFORNIA

ANATOMY OF A BOOK DEAL

Version 1.0

ISBN: 978-0-9819431-8-3

Published by Tinsel Road Books
171 Pier Avenue, #328
Santa Monica, California 90405 USA
www.tinselroad.com

Tinsel Road Books, in association with Global ReLeaf, will plant two trees for each tree used in the manufacturing of its books. Global ReLeaf is an international campaign by American Forests, the nation's oldest nonprofit conservation organization and a world leader in planting trees for environmental restoration.

For my parents, who instilled in me a love of books
at a very very young age.

## DISCLAIMER

This book contains the opinions and ideas of the author. It is intended to provide helpful and informative material designed to help you make informed decisions.

This book is sold with the understanding that the author and publisher are not engaged in rendering legal, financial or any other kind of personal professional services. The reader should consult his agent, attorney or other competent representatives before undertaking a negotiation or pursuing any course of action described in this book or drawing any conclusions from it.

The author and publisher specifically disclaim all responsibility for any liability, loss or risk, personal, professional or otherwise, which may be incurred as a consequence, directly or indirectly, of the use and application of any of the contents of this book

It is not intended as a substitute for proper representation.

# INTRODUCTION

The Anatomy of a Book Deal breaks down in simple terms a typical book deal for a more junior or first time author and explains them within a standard template. We'll explore      the mechanics of an aggressive contract and some of the terms and their effects on an author.  A blank template is also provided for your use. Whether you are an author or publisher, an attorney should be consulted to customize this template to your own circumstances. I won't   be exploring legal minutia in this book. I'll leave that for the attorneys. I also won't be exploring more complicated concepts like multi-book deals nor doing an in depth exploration of subsidiary rights.

This book will make an author more conversant and informed in dealing with their representatives but is not a replacement for proper representation. It always pays to be properly represented. An established representative understands the pitfalls inherent in the      deal making process and also should understand the appetites and the needs of the specific buyer at hand. However, don't settle and don't confuse years of general experience with expertise. Don't assume your own personal attorney can get this done. Attorneys are not one-size fits all in the same way one would not go to a heart surgeon for a knee operation.

I've worked in the entertainment business really since college starting as a concert promoter. I entered the management arena in 1990, advising writers and other intellectual property owners and creators. Since that time, I've done many book deals, the structure and economics of which generally haven't changed for decades, really since the Great Depression.

I've had great clients (both publishers and authors), as well as some clients with very unrealistic expectations of what they were looking to get out of being an author, let alone out of a publishing deal. In 20 years, I've found the worst kind of client is one who lies to themselves about what their own objectives are. Representation helps an author view the process objectively, removing emotion from the equation. Before commencing with any negotiation, each party should have a clear sense of objectives and goals.

# PUBLISHING AGREEMENT

This AGREEMENT is made this MONTH DAY, YEAR (the "Agreement") between PUBLISHING CO, Inc. of ADDRESS (the "Publisher") and AUTHOR NAME (the "Author") c/o AGENT ADDRESS (the "Author's Agent") with respect to a novel currently referred to as NAME OF THE BOOK (the "Work").

This first section of the agreement shows who the contracting parties are and briefly describes what the work is that will be published. Generally a publishing agreement is a form   of license of rights rather than an assignment of rights. It generally isn't a sale of rights. Rights are being lent for a period of time. There are instances where there is transfer of underlying rights such as when a writer is being hired on a work-for-basis or that a partnership has been created but I'll leave those aside for the purposes of this discussion. This will be an exploration of a typical publishing agreement that a first time or a more junior author may be presented with.

In consideration of the parties' promises and obligations as set forth below, the parties agree as follows:

**1.** **RIGHTS GRANTED.** The Author hereby grants and assigns to the Publisher for the full term of copyright, and renewals or extensions thereof, the sole and exclusive right to: (a) print, publish, promote, advertise, distribute and sell the Work in the English language and all other languages throughout the world; and (b) to exercise or authorize the exercise of any of  the other rights in any other form as provided herein.

If the Author is entitled to terminate the grant of any of these rights under the copyright laws of the United States or any other jurisdiction, all other rights transferred or granted hereunder shall remain unaffected by such termination.

> The Rights Granted section would clearly delineate what rights are being conveyed to a publisher. Is it all rights of every kind? Is it just hard cover publishing? The above is a very broad interpretation of rights conveyed to a publisher. There are items that every publisher  will need such as the right to promote, advertise and distribute the work, whatever the "work" is. The word "print" has greater specificity than "publish" which has broad interpretations. This ambiguity however, has led to litigation when the interpretation of what rights have been conveyed has differed between the author and publisher.
>
> Primary rights can and typically include hardcover, trade paperback, mass market and direct mail.  Secondary rights (or subsidiary rights, delineated in more detail below), include,  but are not limited to periodical rights, first and second serial rights (where a publisher can license others to print excerpts of a book prior to publication of the book itself), book club, dramatic rights, film and television rights, videocassette, audio book, radio rights, merchandising (including commercial tie-ins), foreign translation rights among others. Most publishers will minimally seek to acquire hardcover, trade paperback, mass market and direct

mail rights as  part of their primary rights.  In this contract, e-books would be included under electronic rights which are delineated under subsidiary rights. Depending on the situation at hand, an author  may seek to limit the rights (including subsidiary rights) that a publisher may acquire. Whether an author should seek to limit rights or not will come down to the circumstances at hand. This decision should be made in consultation with an author's rep-resentation.

Since technology and new delivery systems continue to advance rapidly, expect the  rights granted to be drafted as broad as possible in favor of the publisher to account for new delivery systems, platforms and versions such as e-books. The burden is on the author to add specificity to these paragraphs defining which rights are granted and which are not.

Included herein is the Term of the deal, which in this case is the duration of the copyright. The term of copyright for works created after 1977 is the author's life plus 70 years. Following the expiration of copyright works go into the public domain where they no longer have copyright protection restricting or limiting the public's use of the work.

Following the Term of the deal, is the definition of the languages publication is granted to the publisher and the territory. Languages may be as narrow as English or as expansive as all languages. The ability for an author to limit or define these languages is likely dictated by the publishing house's appetite for the deal. These rights may be factored into a publishing  house's determination of what an advance may be. The geographic footprint or territory should also be clearly defined. While language does create natural geo-graphic borders, it does remain ambiguous. For instance, if a publisher acquires all English language rights then the deal naturally is multi-national. The same could be said for most of the major languages in the   world.

## 2.     DELIVERY OF THE WORK

**2.1     Elements of the Complete Work.** The Work shall consist of an approximately # of PAGES page manuscript of text. The Author shall prepare and deliver the Work according to the following schedule: the manuscript shall be delivered to the Publisher not later than MONTH DAY, YEAR OF EARLY DELIVERY (the "Early Delivery Date"); and the final, completed manuscript, together with any permissions or clearances and other necessary material shall be delivered to the Publisher not later than MONTH DAY, YEAR OF FINAL DELIVERY (the "Final Delivery Date"). Further, if the Publisher deems an afterward, glossary or some other type of backmatter material necessary for publication of the Work, the Author shall prepare and deliver the requested material by a mutually determined date.

This is where the "Work" itself would be defined. This includes the title, how many pages or words the manuscript has, how many illustrations (if any) etc. It does also explicitly state the schedule for delivery of various elements such as when a draft of a manuscript or other material would be delivered. Permissions and clearances include any releases to use photographs, licensed art work, or licensed lyrics that may be excerpted and included in a work. It is often viewed as the author's burden to acquire permission to use any such elements in the publication of a work. However, an author may negotiate this point with a publisher who may be willing to assume the burden (and possibly the cost) of clearing such elements. If the author is expected to clear works for inclusion, it might benefit the author in time and money to get a necessary release from the publisher to use for such purposes. This will also guarantee that the form and content of the release meets with the publisher's satisfaction.

Early Delivery may be specified as the date that an author is required to deliver an outline, partial manuscript, chapters or a first draft of a work. Final Delivery would be considered the date that all final materials would be delivered to the publisher. This would include the final manuscript and any other materials that may be specified.

Additional deliverables can and often include any mutually agreed Front Matter and Back Matter, the schedule of delivery for which also must be negotiated. Front Matter is the first section of a book and includes any material preceding the main text of a book. This includes (if applicable) a contents, foreword, preface, acknowledgment, introduction, dedication and prologue. Back Matter, if included, includes one or more of the following: epilogue, extro, afterword, conclusion, postscript, appendix, glossary, bibliography, index and colophon. The contract should clearly state which party is responsible for preparing any Front Matter and Back Matter.

**2.2 Acceptable Delivery. (a)** The Author shall deliver the Work and any other materials or information required by this Agreement. It shall be supplied at the Author's own expense, in form and content satisfactory to the Publisher and in accordance with the Text Submission Requirements, the Guidelines for Electronic Manuscripts, and the Submission Requirements for Original Illustrated Art, attached hereto and made a part thereof. Any costs incurred by the Publisher as a result of the Author's failure to meet the specified delivery deadlines or to fulfill the submission requirements shall be charged to the Author, excepting those delays caused by Publisher's requested changes.

To easily facilitate production, each publisher has standardized its own set of delivery requirements. These requirements should be adhered to. These requirements are for the ease of the various production departments. To deviate from the delivery requirements may cause delays throughout an entire production pipeline. If it isn't possible or feasible for an author to deliver in accordance with a publisher's delivery requirements, this should first be dealt with during the contract negotiation. Should an issue arise after signature of a publishing contract, it should be raised and discussed openly with the publisher. Some publishers may be willing to waive portions of delivery requirements based on exigent circumstances. Failure to adhere to production requirements could be viewed by a publisher as "Failure to Deliver" which is covered under paragraph 2.3 below.

**(b)** If permission from others is required for publication of any material contained in the Work, text or visual, or if permission is required for exercise of any other right granted under this Agreement (including without limitation the right to promote the Work), the Author shall secure written permission to reproduce the material throughout the territory in all editions and adaptations of the Work, whether published by the Publisher or its licensees. The Author shall secure such permissions at the Author's own expense and shall submit them, satisfactory to the Publisher in form and content, on the Final Delivery Date specified in Paragraph 2.1. The Author shall consult and cooperate with the Publisher in performing the Author's obligations hereunder.

Authors warrant that material they provide is able to be published. That is to say that it does not infringe on any other party in any way. This includes the author warranting that any photographs, lyrics, drawings or material they provide are cleared and suitable for publication. A contract should be explicit as to which party will clear such materials. A publisher may be willing to assume the burden and cost of obtaining clearances for such materials. Warranties are discussed in further detail below.

**2.3     Failure to deliver.** If the Author fails to deliver the complete and finished manuscript and any permissions and clearances required by the Final Delivery Date, unless otherwise agreed upon in writing by the Publisher, the Publisher may, in its sole discretion, terminate this Agreement upon written notice to the Author, and upon receipt of such notice the Author  shall repay to the Publisher all amounts which may have been advanced under this Agreement within thirty (30) days of receipt of such notice.

Publishers require some remedy in the event an author does not ever deliver the contracted material. In the above, the publisher will make a determination "in its sole discretion" if the delivered material is acceptable in terms of adherence to delivery requirements and often style and substance or content as well. If a manuscript does not meet the delivery requirements then publisher will view that an author has not delivered.

Authors may be able to add a Force Majeure clause which excuses failure to deliver under circumstances that are beyond an author's control such as Acts of God (which includes natural disasters such as hurricanes, earthquakes etc), riots, wars, civil unrest, fire, floods and labor strikes. An author is NOT excused from delivery for any human failure, equipment or computer failures. An exception to this would be if a computer failure was the result of an Act of God or other circumstance beyond the author's control.

**2.4     Right to edit.** The Publisher reserves the right, subject to consultation with the Author, to edit the Work submitted by the Author and to request substituted or additional materials before publication. If the Author fails to supply any of the materials specified by this Agreement, or if any of the materials supplied by the Author are unacceptable to the Publisher, the Publisher shall have the right to supply such materials and charge the cost therefore to the Author.

> Every Publisher will require a right to edit a work submitted by an author. It should be understood that publishing is a collaborative effort and requires real effort from an author. Authors may be able to negotiate a right to approve the editor or have an approval right over the final edited manuscript. It is more common that publishers will consult with authors, retaining business control. In instances where an author may retain an approval right over the edit, a publishing house may have a final right to cancel publication in the event of a disagreement over the edit.

**2.5 Unacceptable delivery.** The Publisher will review the Work and shall notify the Author within sixty (60) days following receipt of the Work whether the material is acceptable or in need of revision. If the Publisher concludes that the Work is unacceptable but could be revised to the Publisher's satisfaction in a timely fashion, the Publisher and the Author shall agree upon the appropriate period of time for the revision process. Should the Publisher determine that the Work as delivered cannot be revised to its satisfaction within a reasonable time period, or if the Publisher determines, in its sole discretion, that the revised manuscript is unacceptable, the Publisher may reject the Work. Upon such rejection, the Publisher shall not be obligated to make any further payments hereunder, and the Author shall use best efforts to sell the Work to another publisher and shall repay to the Publisher any and all sums received under this Agreement out of the first proceeds from such other publisher as and when such monies are received. However, if the Work remains unsold twelve (12) months following rejection, the Author shall promptly repay any and all sums received from the Publisher hereunder. Upon the Publisher's receipt of repayment, the Agreement shall be deemed terminated.

Publishers reserve the right to reject a manuscript that isn't delivered in a manner satisfactory to the publisher. Rejection could result from an array of reasons in addition to not delivering on a timely basis. These include rejection for the quality of the writing or that the submitted work differs in style and substance from what was expected. Publishers may then permit an author to revise the work and resubmit it (as in the above paragraph) "within a reasonable time period."

There is a range of circumstances that may lead a publisher to look to terminate a contract in addition to what it deems may be an unsatisfactory manuscript. These include a change in market conditions. If a publisher can terminate in their "sole discretion," it may have wide latitude in determining whether or not to publish a given work. Above paragraph 2.3 references the author delivering a "complete" manuscript and if author does not in publisher's sole discretion, publisher may terminate the agreement.

Authors may be required to deliver "satisfactory in form and content" which is a much more subjective determination of completeness. If a full manuscript has not been submitted and the author has a publishing agreement prior to a work's completion, the author may wish to attach a synopsis or outline of the work as an exhibit.

Authors should be wary, however, of looking to require or mandate publication. Such a requirement, if a publisher is not invested in the outcome, may result in a mediocre product with no real support within the organization.

Is an advance to be returned to the publisher if a manuscript has been rejected and what is the mechanism for handling it? Typically if a publisher is not publishing a work, then an author will be required to repay any advance they have received. Often the repayment of     an advance will be delayed to permit the author to sell the work to another publisher allowing the publisher to be reimbursed from proceeds received from the second publisher.

**3.      CORRECTIONS. Text Proofs.** The Author shall read, revise, correct, and return all proofs within the reasonable time stipulated by the Publisher. If alterations in the proofs are made at the Author's request (or because of the Author's failure to deliver accurate copy for   the printer) which cost more than ten percent (10%) of the cost of composition, exclusive of   the cost of correcting printers' errors, the Author shall be charged for such excess. The Author shall pay any and all such costs when billed by the Publisher.

> Publisher will generally provide a proof for the author's review. It is expected that authors will review it in a timely basis and make corrections where necessary. In the above, the amount of time for the author to review and make corrections is "stipulated by the publisher." Authors may seek to negotiate specific amounts of time for the review based on their own circumstances. The author may also negotiate to have any agreed upon costs for alterations amounts charged against royalties rather than paid when billed.

**4.      PUBLICATION. (a)** The Publisher shall publish or cause publication of the Work in book form, at the Publisher's own expense, within twelve (12) months of the Publisher's acceptance and approval of the complete and finished Work. The Publisher shall not be responsible for delays caused by force majeure or the act or neglect of a supplier, printer or shipper. In no event shall the Publisher be obligated to publish or cause publication of the Work if, in the Publisher's sole opinion, the Work violates the common law or statutory copyright, or the rights of privacy, publicity, or any other right of any third party or contains libelous or unlawful matter.

This section specifies the outside date that the publisher is required to publish the book following acceptance and approval of the complete work. For the purposes of discussion, 12 months is included. Without a specific timeframe for publication, the author has little recourse in the event that a publisher has not published a book in a sufficiently timely basis. Note the words "acceptance" and "approval." Both are more fully described above, however, until a publisher "accepts" the work, the clock has not begun.

For periodical reviews, the product they often require is a bound review copy of a book 3 to 6 months prior to publication. This often requires having a manuscript that is completed and acceptable to be reviewed and also cover art and establishes a minimum amount of time that a publisher would require to produce, publish and promote a work.

Following delivery, publishers will still retain the right to refrain from publishing works that they determine in their sole opinion that will create liability for the publisher. This includes works that may potentially defame or libel a third party. In the event a publisher declines to publish a work because it may create a liability, author may want to negotiate as to whether author gets to retain any advance or whether it is required to be refunded to the publisher.

Well known or established authors may be able to negotiate contractual commitments related to the promotion and marketing of a book. This includes a publisher potentially committing to the size of a first printing. Also included can be whether any travel fees advanced by a publisher   for promotion and marketing can be charged back to an author.

**(b)** Decisions regarding the title, format, interior design, and cover for the Work, and all other design, production and publishing decisions are within the Publisher's sole discretion. It is specifically understood and agreed that the Publisher shall own and control any and all rights to any design for the Work created or commissioned by the Publisher, and the Author may not duplicate such design without the Publisher's express prior written consent.

> As you'll notice, approvals are omitted from this contract. It is unlikely that authors will be offered approval rights of any significance. Approvals may certainly be negotiated. Publishers will usually look to retain the right to change the title of a work, determine the design of a cover and all other aspects of design and formatting. Exceptions to this are cases where authors or licensors own an existing brand or venerable brands as is the case with movie studios licensing film tie-ins.

**5.     FAILURE TO PUBLISH.** Provided the Author delivers the Work in accordance   with the delivery dates and requirements specified herein, if the Publisher has not published or caused publication of the Work within the time specified, unless publication has been delayed due to circumstances beyond the Publisher's reasonable control, the Author may give the Publisher written notice of the Author's desire to terminate this Agreement, and if the Publisher then fails to publish the Work within six (6) months following receipt of such notice, this Agreement shall terminate, and the Author shall retain any advances previously received under this Agreement in full settlement of all claims against Publisher.

While paragraph 2.5 provides remedy and recourse for the publisher should an author not deliver, this crucial paragraph provides recourse to the author. The mechanism for the rights to revert to the author in the event the publisher fails to publish should be clearly delineated.

**6.     COPYRIGHT. (a)** The Publisher shall register the copyright in the Work in the United States Copyright Office in the name of NAME OF COPYRIGHT HOLDER and shall ensure that each copy of the Work published by Publisher contains a copyright notice in such names pursuant to the United States Copyright Act and the Universal Copyright Convention, together with such other notices as the Author may request in writing.

As mentioned above, for works created after 1977, the duration of copyright runs the term of the author's life plus 70 years. There are exceptions to this such as made-for-hire works where a corporation is the copyright holder. For the sake of ease and brevity, we'll again focus on a more traditional publishing agreement between a first time or more junior author and a publisher. It is an issue that first time authors generally need not be concerned about. A copyright is a long term asset, one that bestows rights on the owner and may be even used as collateral.  The publisher will customarily register the work for copyright in the United States    in addition to other countries that the publisher may be licensing the work on behalf of the author or copyright owner.
If a publisher is supplying individual elements of a book such as cover artwork, they may look to retain copyright over their own work product.

**(b)** Upon the Publisher's request, the Author shall execute any such papers and documents which the Publisher may deem advisable to protect, assign, record, renew, or otherwise perfect or enforce the rights in and to the Work granted to the Publisher hereunder.

Requiring any additional documents is a standard provision. Publishing houses will look to protect any rights it may have in a work. Some publishers may look to be designated as an author's "attorney-in-fact" where the publisher is empowered to sign documents on an author's behalf if the author is unable to do so on a timely basis. Authors can receive some extra protection in this paragraph by requiring that all additional documents shall be "consistent herewith" or consistent with the agreement at hand.

7.      **ADVANCE.**   Subject to terms and conditions of this Agreement, the Publisher shall pay to the Author, as a non-returnable advance against and on account of all monies accruing to the Author under this Agreement, the sum of NUMBER OF DOLLARS (US $XXXX) payable as follows:

An Advance is just that, an advance against royalties. It should clearly state that the advance is non-returnable otherwise a publisher could require an author to return any monies that haven't been earned out.

Advances are often determined by a simple profit and loss analysis. They are not a measure of an editor's love or commitment to the material. This analysis is conducted in consultation with each department involved in production and sale of a book. This includes sales reps who often will check in with buyers at key accounts and evaluate market circumstances. If an author has no track record, then comparable books may be studied to begin to come up with a sales picture.

Advances are often paid in steps or installments, with a first portion often being paid   on signature and a portion being paid on delivery of certain materials. These installments are subject to negotiation between the parties and may be dictated by publisher appetite. This is done to provide a publisher with some recourse for an author not delivering material. A general rule of thumb is that many publishers will pay an advance equal to what an author is estimated to earn in the book's first year of exploitation. Typically the larger the advance the greater the commitment the publisher will be required to make to selling the book to earn back its investment. The contract should clearly delineate the advance and when it is to be paid. In the above paragraph, the advance is "against and on account of all monies accruing to the Author." This provides for all subsidiary rights sales and all sales of every kind to be used to recoup the advance.

$XXXX within thirty (30) days following the receipt by Publisher of a fully executed Agreement.

In the above, the publisher will pay the advance to Author when it has received a   signed agreement from the author and it itself has signed the agreement. The remaining milestones below may or may not be included and are subject to negotiation between the author and publisher.

$XXXX within thirty (30) days following the Publisher's receipt and acceptance of all material due the Publisher upon the Early Delivery Date.

$XXXX within thirty (30) days following the Publisher's receipt and acceptance of all material due the Publisher upon the Final Delivery Date.

$XXXX within thirty (30) days following the Publisher's first publication of the Work.

**8.** **ROYALTIES.** Royalties on the Publisher's editions of the Work shall be based upon the net retail sales, less a reasonable reserve for returnable copies, and paid at the following rates:

Royalties often vary by type of edition, with paperbacks typically being a royalty lower than hardcover. On a hard cover book, an author may receive approximately 10% (or even less for first time authors) of the list or retail price on the first five or ten thousand units sold at the retail price, which would escalate to 12.5% of retail on the next five thousand, further escalating to 15% of retail thereafter. This royalty would decrease to approximately 7.5% of retail on trade paperbacks. This does not mean that an author may not be able to be successful in negotiating royalties that are greater than the above.

With a brand with weight or real buyer appetite, an author may be able to negotiate bonuses based on successes such as inclusion on the New York Times best seller list. In one instance representing a venerable brand, we were able to achieve a bonus for each week the work appeared at #1 on the Times List of an additional advance of $7,500 per week. Further, for each week the Work appeared in positions 2 through 5 the brand owner was to be paid a sum of $5,000 and for each week the work appeared in positions 6 through 15 the brand owner was to be paid the sum of $2,500. This was all an advance against royalties and with a cap of $15,000 under the bonus section.

Note that the above references a "reasonable reserve for returnable copies." It does not though establish what "reasonable" is nor how long said reserve would be held by a publisher. Publishing houses vary in practice. It generally does not favor the author to have a fixed percentage of sales for a reserve for returns. A fixed percentage may unduly penalize an author when a publisher is aware that the majority of returns have in fact been accounted for. Author may look to negotiate a period of time that a reserve may be held before requiring it to be released to the author.

**(a)**     On copies of a hardcover edition sold in the United States, except as described in subparagraphs (d) through (f) below:

>A% of the suggested retail price on the first F copies sold;
>B% of the suggested retail price on the next G copies sold;
>C% of the suggested retail price on the next H copies sold;
>D% of the suggested retail price on the next I copies sold; and
>E% of the suggested retail price on all copies sold thereafter.

>Royalties may escalate based on levels of success. This is typically an escalating percentage of the retail price. Escalations would occur at thresholds of units sold.

**(b)**     On copies of a paperback edition sold in the United States, except as described in subparagraphs (d) through (f) below:

>X% of the suggested retail price on all copies sold.

**(c)**     On copies of a board back edition sold in the United States, except as described in subparagraphs (d) through (f) below:

>X% of the suggested retail price on all copies sold.

> Board book editions are often only applicable with kids picture books and the like.

**(d)** On all copies sold: at a discount of 51% or higher, for special or premium use sales; for export or sale outside the United States; or as a result of the Publisher's mail-order efforts, through couponed advertising, or circulation direct to the customer: 10% of the net amounts received by the Publisher.

> Publishers will seek to pay lower royalties on special sales which traditional necessitate deep discounting on their part. This includes sales to book clubs, school editions, and mail order sales.

**(e)** On copies of any edition sold by the Publisher from any reprinting of X thousand (X) copies or less made at least one (1) year after the date of initial publication of the Work: one-half (1/2) of prevailing U.S. rate for that edition based upon cover price.

**(f)** No royalties shall be payable on copies or adaptations of the Work or on ancillary products which are distributed for purposes of promotion or advertising; on copies sold below the Publisher's cost; on portions of the Work sublicensed for publicity use without compensation; or on copies provided to the Author free of charge.

> Publishers won't want to be obligated to pay royalties on copies that are given away for promotional purposes or copies on which they will lose money (as in the above "sold below the Publisher's cost").

**9.    SUBSIDIARY RIGHTS. (a)** Pursuant to Paragraph 1, the Author's grant to the Publisher includes the sole and exclusive right to sell or license the Work for use as follows in any language throughout the world upon such terms as the Publisher deems advisable. Except as otherwise specified, the net proceeds of such sales or licenses shall be divided between the Author and the Publisher as follows:

Subsidiary rights are all rights that are adjacent to or secondary to the initial publishing rights granted. This can includes nook club, foreign publication, translation, serial rights, reprint rights, other book formats, storage, audio book, ancillary, merchandising and performance rights. Each publisher's business model will vary and those models will dictate which Subsidiary Rights will be a give on their part and which won't.

|  | Publisher's Share | Author's Share |
|---|---|---|
| Book club (whether in full length, condensed, or abridged version) | 50% | 50% |

Book club books are often printed by book clubs themselves under license from the publisher. These books are often be sold at a significant discount.

|  | Publisher's Share | Author's Share |
|---|---|---|
| Foreign publication (which may include the right of such licensee to sublicense certain subsidiary rights in that market) | 50% | 50% |
| Translation (which may include the right of such licensee to sub-license certain subsidiary rights in that market) | 50% | 50% |

Foreign publication and Translation rights may be able to be reserved by author depending on publisher's and the market's appetite for a given title. These rights may be factored into a profit and loss analysis that was used to determine an author's potential advance. By retaining these rights author's may be able to license to firms separately where any advances on a territory by territory basis will not be crossed collateralized. That is to say the gains from one territory will not be used to offset the losses from another.

| | | |
|---|---|---|
| Serial (use of serializations, condensations, excerpts, digests, etc. of text and/or images in newspapers, magazines, other periodicals, books or pamphlets) | 50% | 50% |
| Reprint (whether in full length, condensed, or abridged version) | 50% | 50% |
| Other Book Publication (including, but not limited to, deluxe editions, large print and direct mail editions) | 50% | 50% |
| Storage, retrieval, microfilm, microfiche, other forms of electronic reproduction | 50% | 50% |

Many publishers are either having a separately delineated royalty for e-books or they are including them in the broad definition of electronic reproduction. Since publishers are releasing e-books themselves rather than licensing to third parties, under the scenario of including e-books under electronic reproduction, the last paragraph of this section would become applicable and a deal between the parties would "be subject to mutual agreement between the parties."

| | | |
|---|---|---|
| Ancillary Products (i.e. book – or | 50% | 50% |

stationary-related product that uses
text and/or images from the Work,
including without limitation books
(e.g. blank or specialty books), stamp
kits, calendars, postboxes, stationery,
bulk notecards and notecard collections,
postcards and postcard collections, day
books, address books, posters, magnets,
gift wrap, photo albums, and photo frames)

| | | |
|---|---|---|
| Merchandising: including but not limited to the use of title, text, and/or images to create or promote commercial products | 50% | 50% |

Merchandising is fairly straight forward. If the publisher commissioned and owns the artwork used for the cover of a book, the cover artwork is often intertwined with a merchandising program. Few literary agencies have departments to administer merchandising and licensing programs which are often viewed as brand extensions of a book. In success, merchandising can be a very significant source of revenue for brands with merchandising potential. If an author seeks to license film and/or television rights, there may be real incentive to allow the publisher to administer "book based merchandising" which would be merchandising based on imagery in a book in contrast to actor's likeness which would be merchandised from a film. If an author retained merchandising and sold entertainment rights, the movie or television studio would look to acquire merchandising as part of the property for no additional fee.

| | | |
|---|---|---|
| Performance: TV, radio, sight and sound, and allied rights, visual | 50% | 50% |

reproduction, motion picture,
dramatic and non dramatic

> If performance rights are going to be conveyed then a publisher should be expected to be able to demonstrate a track record and success in licensing such rights. For an author to retain any subsidiary rights but not have the ability to sell them or relationships to maximize them could be contradictory to the potential growth of a brand. Simply, it's often better to have 50% of something rather than 100% of nothing. That said, in the success of a book and brand, all reserved rights continue to increase in value.

If the Publisher exercises any of the foregoing rights itself instead of licensing others to do so, the royalty rates, where not otherwise specified in Paragraph 8 above, shall be subject to mutual agreement between the parties.

**10.     AUTHOR'S COPIES.** The Publisher shall give to the Author, on first publication, fifteen (15) free copies of the hardcover edition of the Work published by the Publisher. The Publisher agrees to ship all such free copies at the Publisher's expense. In addition, the Author shall have the right to purchase copies of the Work at the following discounts for prepaid orders: forty percent (40%) on orders of 1 to 24 copies; fifty percent (50%) on orders of 25 copies or more. All such discounted copies of the Work purchased by the Author shall be shipped at the Author's expense. Copies of the Work provided to the Author under the terms of this Paragraph shall not be resold. All sales of books by the Publisher to the Author are subject to applicable sales tax.

> The Author will generally receive an allotment of copies that are for his or her personal use. Following the allotment the author is typically permitted to purchase copies at a discount. The discount off of retail may be

negotiable by the author, however, publisher will look to not lose money in selling discounted copies to the author. Author copies are not generally intended for re-sale by the author.

**11.    PUBLICITY. (a)** The Publisher, and any of its licensees or assigns hereunder, shall have the right to use the Author's name, image, likeness, and biography in connection with the exercise of any of such rights, and in advertising and publicity in connection therewith. The Publisher shall provide the Author with an Author Questionnaire, which the Author shall complete and return by a date to be specified by the Publisher. It is understood and agreed that the Author shall provide at the Author's expense a reproducible photograph of the Author that the Publisher may use in connection with the Work and in advertising and promotion of the Work. Any photograph provided by the Author will be deemed approved by the Author. The Author shall cooperate, at the Publisher's expense, in advertising and promotional activities as reasonably requested by the Publisher. The Author shall not compete with the Publisher in promotion and sale of the Work. Notwithstanding anything in the foregoing to the contrary, the Publisher shall obtain the Author's prior written approval before using the Author's name, image, likeness, biography, or the title or any element of the Work in connection with products or services not appropriate for children (e.g. cigarettes, alcohol, condoms, etc.).

This section simply provides for the publicity of the Work, granting the publisher use of the author's name, image, likeness and biography in connection with the book itself. Authors may be able to "approve" their image, likeness and biography however in the above the author is provided an opportunity to submit their own photograph for publisher's use. Accordingly the publisher has the expectation that whatever photograph an author would submit for publisher's use would be suitable to the author.

A questionnaire typically would aid the publisher in crafting talking points for a promotional campaign.

**(b)** For publicity or promotion purposes, the Publisher may permit, subject to consultation with the Author, the broadcast (but not dramatization) by radio or television or on-line, without charge, such selections from the Work as in the opinion of the Publisher may benefit from the sale of the Work. Failure of the Publisher to consult with the Author under this subparagraph 11(b) shall not be deemed a material breach of this Agreement.

> The above section provides for the promotion of the work on television, radio or on-line. This is a result of an adjacency to rights that may be reserved to the author or are specifically addressed under subsidiary rights. This grants the publisher the right to promote the work using selections such as chapters that may be placed on-line or read on radio.

**12.  ACCOUNTING AND PAYMENT. (a)** The Publisher shall render semi-annual statements of account to December 31 and June 30 of each year, on or before March 31 and September 30 following, and shall send such statements, together with payment of the amounts due thereon. For each royalty period, the Publisher may withhold a reasonable reserve against returns of books. After two (2) years following the original publication date, if the accumulated earnings from all sources for the Work do not exceed twenty-five dollars ($25), the Publisher may defer a statement and payment until such time as the accumulated earnings for the Work total twenty-five dollars ($25) or more; however, upon the Author's request, the Publisher shall render a statement, regardless of amount due. Should the Author receive an overpayment, it is understood and agreed that the Publisher may deduct such amount from any further earnings of the Work.

Authors will want to negotiate explicit payment terms whether quarterly, semi-annually or annually. This includes when statements are due and also when which the related amounts are to be paid. Most publishers generate all of their accounting reports at set periods of time. For newer authors, publishers may be unwilling (or unable) to generate reports on a more frequent basis than they may be able to administratively handle. Authors may be able to negotiate additional terms such as a reversion in the event of a failure by the publisher to account and provide statements. Unless there is a significant appetite on the part of the buyer, it's unlikely that more junior or first time authors will be able modify this section significantly.

**(b)** The Publisher shall pay the Author's share of the proceeds from the sale or license of subsidiary rights as provided in Paragraph 9, less any unearned advances or other debits to the Author's royalty account, within sixty (60) days following the Publisher's receipt of such monies.

**(c )** The Author may, upon written request, examine or cause to be examined through certified public accountants or the Author's qualified representative the Publisher's books of account to the extent that they relate to the sale or licensing of the Work, provided such examinations are limited to one (1) per year and take place during regular business hours. Such examination shall be at the Author's expense; however, if errors of accounting totaling ten percent (10%) or more of the total sums due the Author hereunder are found and agreed to be to the Author's disadvantage, the Publisher shall reimburse the Author for the reasonable out-of-pocket costs of such examination up to the amount of the error.

Authors may be able to strengthen an audit right. In the above paragraph, if there's an error "totaling ten percent (10%) or more," the "Publisher shall reimburse the Author

for reasonable out-of-pocket costs of such examination."
This may be able to be modified to 5% subject to the
circumstances at hand.  Prior to pursuing any audit, an
author should discuss the cost and potential benefits with
their accountant and other representatives.

Often publishers will include a clause providing
that if a statement is not contested within a specific period
of time, it becomes binding and may not be audited in the
future. This also serves to limit the period of time an author
may be able to bring a legal case.

**13.    AUTHOR'S WARRANTIES. (a)** The Author represents,
warrants and covenants that (i) the Author is the sole author of the
Work; (ii) the Author is the sole owner of all rights granted
hereunder; (iii) the Author has not sold, licensed, assigned, or
otherwise encumbered the Work, and will not sell, license, assign, or
otherwise encumber, any of such rights; (iv) the Author has the full
power to enter into and to perform this Agreement; (v) except for
material expressly permitted or cleared pursuant to the provisions of
Paragraph 2.2(b), all text, illustrations, and other material contained
in the Work is original, previously unpublished, and is not in the
public domain, whether as defined under the United States
Copyright Act or otherwise; and (vi) the Work in no way violates
any copyright or proprietary or contract or personal right of others,
including the right of privacy and that it contains nothing unlawful
or libelous. The foregoing warranties shall be in effect throughout
the term of this Agreement and shall survive its termination.

Author will be required to make an array of
warranties that relate to the originality of the material and
that the publication does not infringe on any third party.
While the warranties are not highly negotiable, authors may
be able to modify this paragraph slightly so that the
warranty covers only material that the author provides and
that the warranties are "to the best of Author's knowledge."

If the work is a cook book or similar book of instructions, authors will be expected to warrant that there are no errors or omissions in any recipe, formula or set of instructions.

**(b) Publisher's verification of warranties.** The Publisher shall have no obligation to make an independent investigation to determine whether the foregoing warranties and representations are true, and any such investigation by or for the Publisher shall not constitute a defense to the Author in any action based upon a breach or alleged breach of any of the foregoing representations or warranties of the Author. However, if in the Publisher's reasonable opinion there appears to be a substantial risk of liability to third persons or entities or of governmental action against the Work, the Publisher with the Author's agreement may undertake an investigation, verification and analysis of the Work and implement such revisions of the Work with the approval of the Author which Publisher believes may eliminate or lessen such risk. Notwithstanding anything to the contrary contained herein, in no event shall Publisher be obliged to publish the Work if in its judgment the Work contains libelous material, or its publication would violate the rights of privacy, copyright, or any other rights of any person or entity.

> Publishers tend to operate on the assurances given by the author. It is generally cost prohibitive to separately verify each release or warranty given by an author. Publishers, like most corporations, are loathe to assume unnecessary risk or liability. If a publisher determines that publishing a given work will result in liability, it will likely look to limit said liability. This often results in a publisher refraining from publishing said work.

14.     **INDEMNITY. (a)** In the event of any claim, demand, suit, action or proceeding ("Claim") based upon an alleged breach of the Author's warranties, the Publisher shall have     the right to select

counsel to defend itself and the Author, and the Author shall indemnify and hold harmless the Publisher, any seller of the Work, any licensee of a subsidiary right in the Work, and any other person to whom the Publisher or its licensees may extend the representations and warranties contained herein in connection with the production or distribution of the Work or the exercise of any rights therein or derived therefrom, against any losses, damages and expenses (including reasonable legal fees and expenses) arising or resulting from or in connection with any such Claim. The Author shall cooperate fully in the defense of any such Claim, and acknowledges that failure to cooperate in the defense of any Claim shall be deemed a breach of this Agreement. If the Author so chooses, the Author may join in the defense of any Claim with an attorney of the Author's own choosing at the Author's own expense. The Publisher may settle any such Claim against it or waive any appeal of any judgment of a trial court against it. If such Claim is successfully defended or is settled, the Author's indemnity hereunder shall be limited to fifty percent (50%) of the cost of defense and the amount of settlement (if any). Any and all monies awarded to the Publisher in association with a successful defense or settlement shall be shared equally between the Publisher and the Author after the Publisher first recovers its real costs and expenses associated with such defense or settlement.

Authors may be able to be included on a publisher's errors and omissions insurance policy as an additional insured. This should place a limit on any financial exposure that an author may have in the event of a claim or suit against the publisher related to the exploitation of the work. The author may further be able to limit his or her liability to limiting exposure to breaches, removing claims all together or removing the word "alleged." This would redefine a claim to a breach that would require proven rather than merely asserted.

Other issues that require consideration include whether the publisher can withhold royalties on account to offset legal expenses? Is there interest paid to author on any money withheld? Does the publisher have the ability to settle a claim without prior approval of the author? Is there a financial limitation on an amount of settlement without author approval or prior approval?

**(b)** If a Claim is instituted, the party receiving notice of the Claim shall promptly notify the other in writing and shall give the fullest information obtainable at the time of such Claim. Upon receipt of any Claim which would obligate the Author under the above indemnity, the Publisher reserves the right to withhold amounts otherwise payable to the Author and to apply such amounts (as required) in satisfaction of the foregoing indemnities. In addition to any other rights in law and equity, in the event of any material breach by the Author of the Author's warranties, the Publisher may as a final remedy terminate this Agreement and recover any monies advanced to the Author under this Agreement. The foregoing indemnities shall survive the termination of this Agreement.

**15.    DEFENSE OF COPYRIGHT.** In case of any infringement of the copyright of the Work by others, the Publisher may in its discretion sue or employ such remedies as it deems expedient, and all such suits or proceedings shall be at the joint expense of the Author and the Publisher, and the net proceeds of any recovery shall be divided equally between them, but the Author shall not be liable for any expenditure for such purposes in excess of one thousand dollars ($1,000) undertaken by the Publisher without the Author's previous consent in writing, such costs shall be charged to Author's royalty account. If the Author does not consent to all expenditures for such purposes, any recovery shall be divided between the Publisher and the Author in the ratio of their respective expenditures for such purposes. The Author authorizes the Publisher to join as a plaintiff or co-plaintiff in any litigation against one or more third parties for infringement of the copyright in the Work, without cost to the Author, except as provided by this Paragraph.

**16.     COMPETITIVE MATERIAL. (a)** During the term of this Agreement, (i) the Author shall not, without the Publisher's prior written consent, publish or authorize publication by anyone other than the Publisher of any edition or adaptation, abridgment or condensation of the Work or any derivative work (including without limitation, any screenplay, television script, novelization or photonovel); and (ii) the Author will not publish or authorize publication of   any similar material in book, article or pamphlet form, or ancillary product which is likely to directly compete with the sale of the Work.

> This paragraph would effectively preclude an author from publishing, creating or authorizing any similar material or ancillary product that may directly compete with the sale of the book. Authors may have the ability to define more specifically what competitive material is and what the term is for the non-compete. Authors may be able to put an outside date on the non compete clause.

**(b)** The Author shall not contribute more than 300 words from the Work to any one book, pamphlet or magazine without the Publisher's prior written approval. Further, the Author's name shall not appear on the cover of any other book on the same subject as the Work.

> If a publishing house is going to invest their resources in launching a book and author, typically they will look to prevent the author from publishing works with other publishers that will compete directly with the Work. These limitations may have a defined scope as to subject matter. An author may be able to limit or more narrowly

define this section. Authors may be able to negotiate an outside date following which it may publish material which is competitive with the Work. Publishers will look to prevent authors from publishing sequels or other material with the same characters with other publishers.

**17.    AUTHOR'S PROPERTY.** The Author shall retain complete copies of all materials provided by the Author to the Publisher for the Work. In the event of loss or damage to the copies delivered to the Publisher, the Publisher's liability shall be limited to the cost of making an additional set of copies if such materials from the set retained by the Author. Except for the loss or damage caused by the Publisher's negligent acts or omissions, the Publisher shall not be responsible for the loss of or damage to any of the Author's property. The Publisher's liability for loss of or damage to any such property shall in no event exceed One Hundred Dollars ($100) for any duplicate slide, Two Hundred Fifty Dollars ($250) for any original transparency or One Thousand Dollars ($1,000) for any original illustration, but in no event shall the Publisher's total liability exceed Ten Thousand Dollars ($10,000). Should the Author require insurance in excess of Ten Thousand Dollars ($10,000), a rider for the excess can be established at the Author's expense.

> While it's nearly impossible to put a value on intangible creative property, one must   put a value on hard assets so they may be insured. An author or artist should not send a publisher originals of any material and should maintain multiple archived copies of all files and creative assets. This paragraph is designed to protect both an author and a publisher in the event of damage or loss of an author's property.

**18.    OPTION.** The Author shall offer the Publisher the opportunity to acquire the same rights as are herein granted with respect to the Author's next book length work for GENRE in the style and substance of the Work, before submitting it to any other publisher whether directly or indirectly. The Publisher shall be entitled to a period of four (4) weeks after submission of such next work within which to notify the Author of Publisher's decision, which period shall in no event commence to run prior to one (1) month after the Publisher's initial publication of the Work hereunder. If within that period the Publisher shall notify the Author of its desire to publish the manuscript, the Publisher shall thereupon negotiate with the Author with respect to the terms of such publication. If the parties are unable to agree upon the terms within thirty (30) business days after the Author's receipt of the Publisher's offer, the Author shall be free to submit the manuscript elsewhere.

Most publishing houses will ask for an option on a newer author's next work. The author may be able (and want) to limit an option to the same specific genre of the work at hand. For instance, if an author's book is a young adult novel then the author may want to limit an option to young adult material rather than include other books such as cookbooks etc.

Publishers will look to place limitations on an author's ability to submit works. A publisher isn't looking to be forced into a decision making process prior to the author's first book even being released. While an author is not precluded from submitting works in the above, the period of time the publisher has to review a next work does not commence until one month after publication of the work at hand.

The type of option offered may vary by publisher. As in the above, authors may be offered a first look that provides for an exclusive period of review followed by an exclusive negotiation period. There is an extensive array of variations of options in addition to a first look including last refusal (the publisher can match the terms that an author is willing to accept   from another publisher), first refusal (provides for a publisher to acquire a book on specified terms) and first look with a last refusal (same provisions as first look but in the event no deal   is reached an author may submit the work in question elsewhere. In the event the author receives an offer from another publisher, the author must offer the material to the publisher on the same terms.)

Is the current agreement used as a floor requiring the writer to offer publisher the same rights on the same terms or are the rights and terms negotiable? The above paragraph provides that an author is required to offer the publisher to acquire the same rights as those included in the agreement at hand. The ability of an author to modify or eliminate an option will depend on the author's negotiating strength. The number of days that the parties negotiate may potentially be decreased by an author and is subject to an agreement. Thirty days is a typical negotiating  period for a negotiation right.

If the initial book is part of a series, publishers may want to wait and gauge the success of the first book before committing to a second book in a series.

**19.     TERMINATION OF THIS AGREEMENT. (a) Out of print.** If the Work is out of print, and the Publisher does not agree to bring out a new printing or has entered into a sublicense for a reprint edition within six (6) months following receipt of the Author's written notice (unless delayed by circumstances beyond the Publisher's control), this Agreement shall terminate and all rights granted to the Publisher shall revert to the Author upon written request, subject to Publisher's continued participation in any licenses granted by the Publisher.

Authors will want a mechanism for termination of the grant of rights in the event that the work is no longer being published. Authors may request that the work is either printed in a new printing or sub-licensed. If this doesn't occur within an agreed upon number of months then the rights may revert. Authors may have latitude to decrease the number of months allowing for the practicality of a publisher to reprint a work.

**(b) Discontinuance.** If at any time after first publication, the Publisher wishes to discontinue publication for any reason, the Publisher may do so upon written notice to the Author, in which event this Agreement shall terminate and all rights granted hereunder shall revert to the Author upon the termination date set forth in such notice from the Publisher.

> In most instances, publishers may discontinue publication of the Work in its sole discretion. This also may serve to terminate the grant of rights.

**(c) Remainders.** The Publisher may, in its sole discretion, offer copies of the Work for sale as "remainders" at any price it sees fit. The royalty payable upon copies sold as remainders shall be ten (10%) of the amount received, less manufacturing costs, and shall not exceed any other royalty rate set forth in this Agreement. The Publisher shall notify the Author prior to such remaindering and shall offer the Author the opportunity to purchase copies at the estimated remainder price, plus shipping and handling; however, any inadvertent failure to do so shall not be deemed a breach of this Agreement.

> Remainders are essentially remaining copies that a publisher was not able to sell and it is therefore required to significantly discount them. Remaindering is often preferred to pulping a remaining stock of inventory.

**(d) Printer's materials.** For thirty (30) days after the date of such termination, the Author shall have the right, but not the obligation, to purchase any printer's materials under the Publisher's control, at the fair market value thereof. If the Author does not exercise such right within thirty (30) days, the Publisher may dispose of any such materials without further obligation to the Author.

> Following a termination, an author may or may not want to acquire materials from the publisher. Materials can include layouts, pre-press files or plates, and cover artwork among other items.

## 20.    TERMINATION UNDER U.S. COPYRIGHT LAW.

If, pursuant to the United States Copyright Act, the Author (of, if deceased, the successor of the Author) has the right to terminate the rights granted hereunder, and elects to exercise such rights as provided pursuant to such Act, after such termination, the Author shall not exercise or dispose of such rights except in accordance with the following procedure: commencing with the date of such termination, the Author and the Publisher shall negotiate in good faith for a period of not less than sixty (60) days with respect to mutually agreeable terms and conditions. If the parties are unable in good faith to arrive at a mutually satisfactory agreement for such publication, the Author shall be free to offer the rights terminated elsewhere, provided, however, that prior to entering into any agreement with any such third party, the Author shall first give the Publisher the opportunity to agree, within ten (10) business days, to match the terms offered by such third party which the Author is willing to accept.

## 21.    GOVERNING LAW.

Regardless of the place of its actual execution and performance, this Agreement shall be treated as though executed and performed within the State of California, and shall be governed by and interpreted under the laws of the State of California.

The governing law will typically be whatever state the publisher (or its parent company) is based in. It's unlikely that a publisher will cede governing law to an author.

**22.    COMPLETE AGREEMENT, MODIFICATION, AND INTERPRETATION.** This Agreement constitutes the complete understanding of the parties, and no waivers or modifications of any provision shall be valid unless in writing, signed by the Author and the Publisher. This Agreement supersedes any prior agreements between the parties with regard to its subject matter, whether oral or written. The waiver of a breach or of a default under any provision hereof shall not be deemed a waiver or any subsequent breach or default. The payment of any advances or royalties hereunder shall not be deemed a waiver by the Publisher of any rights and/or claims that it may have with respect to nonperformance by the Author of the Author's obligations hereunder. The language of this Agreement shall in all cases be construed in accordance with its full and fair meaning.

This is a standard paragraph and typically does not require many changes. Rights conveyed are often reciprocal.

**23.    ASSIGNMENT.** This Agreement shall be binding upon and shall inure to the benefit of the respective parties, their heirs, executors, administrators, successors and assigns, and may not be assigned by either party without the other's written consent, except that the Publisher may, without the Author's consent, assign this Agreement to its parent, or any subsidiary or affiliated company, or to any company which acquires all or substantially all of its assets.

In today's climate both parties will want and expect assignment language. An author will want to be able to assign the income and publishing agreement to their heirs or estate. Similarly a corporation will want the ability to assign the agreement to parent companies or affiliates.

**24.    NOTICES.** Any and all notices or other communications required or permitted by this Agreement shall be in writing and shall be deemed delivered when personally delivered to the party to whom it is addressed, or in lieu of such personal delivery, five (5) business days after deposit in the United States mail, first class, postage prepaid, addressed to such party at the appropriate address as set forth in this Agreement. Either party may change its address by written notice of such change delivered in accordance with this Paragraph.

This is a standard notices paragraph with mutual parameters for delivery of notices to the other party. Authors may look to add other provisions that include a clause defining how publishing rights are treated in the event of bankruptcy of the publisher. A mediation or arbitration clause provides for dispute resolution among the parties. Mediation or arbitration may be a more cost effective means of resolving a conflict than pursuing other legal remedies.

An Agency clause may be added to provide that the agency negotiating on behalf of the author shall be paid under this deal in perpetuity and the direction of such payments may not   be revoked by the author. This is common in the publishing industry and should be expected.

IN WITNESS WHEREOF, the parties have duly executed this Agreement the day and year last written below.

AUTHOR                              NAME OF PUBLISHER

_____          _____

Author's name                          Signature of Publisher

_____

Print Name

_____          _____

Date                                    Date

_____

Author's Agent's Tax ID Number

## TEXT SUBMISSION REQUIREMENTS

As discussed above, every publisher will delineate the style and manner that a manuscript should be delivered. This will specify if delivery is electronic and what word processing programs may be acceptable.

Form of manuscript. Author shall deliver the manuscript in the English language to NAME OF PUBLISHER ("Publisher") as readable CD-Rom(s) in a word-processing program approved by Publisher, and two (2) complete letter-quality printouts of the entire disc. The manuscript shall be clean and legibly typed and double-spaced with numbered pages. If the manuscript is not in satisfactory form, Publisher may have it retyped and organize it at Author's expense. The accompanying computer disc must follow the guidelines specified below. Author will input all editorial changes onto this disc.

Contents of manuscript. The complete manuscript shall include the following elements: title page; dedication page; preface, foreword, and/or introduction; acknowledgements including credits, if applicable; table of contents; list of illustrations, if applicable; captions, if applicable; text with headings, part titles, and/or chapter titles as needed; an index, if required; and permissions and releases.

Factual Accuracy. The complete manuscript shall be as accurate and factually up-to-date as current information systems allow. For all manuscripts: proper name of people, places, and titles; all statistical and historical information; dates; and permissions must be properly spelled and factually correct. For regional, foreign, and other travel and/or guide books: all of the preceding requirements apply and phone numbers, addresses, directions, fees, and hours of operation must be current and accurate. If the manuscript is deemed factually incorrect at delivery, Publisher may hire fact-checking services at Author's expense.

Quotations and/or sources. All shall be accurate, and the spelling and wording of institutional, corporate, or other proper names shall be correct.

Part titles, chapter titles, and headings. All shall be typed in capital and lower case letters. Part titles should be typed on separate manuscript pages and numbered in sequence with the rest of the text. Headings should be consistent in form throughout the manuscript, though some distinction should be made among different types of headings.

Recipes. Recipes shall be submitted according to the Recipe Guidelines attached.

Bibliography. All entries shall be alphabetized by authors' surnames and form of the information included should be consistent.

Glossary. All entries shall be arranged alphabetically, with the defined term underlined.

Page numbers. All pages shall be numbered.

Photographs, Illustrations, Charts or Graphs. All artwork shall be numbered for identification and, if accompanying specific text, the manuscript must also be cross-referenced to indicate where the appropriate artwork should appear.

Captions. Captions shall be listed separately and each caption identified by the photograph or illustration number it corresponds to. Any credits for photographs or illustrations shall also be typed on a separate page and each credit marked with the corresponding image number.

Author shall also include a letter or memorandum summarizing the contents of the package, noting any offbeat punctuation, unusual spelling, or other areas to which Publisher should pay special attention. See note below about the "insert symbol" function: please call it to our attention when it is used for unusual symbols or spelling in the manuscript.

# GUIDELINES FOR ELECTRONIC MANUSCRIPTS

The manuscript should be submitted on a CD-Rom disc readable by IBM-compatible or Mac computer programs. A manuscript prepared on an electronic typewriter with a disc (a dedicated word processor, such as a Brother, Smith-Corona, etc) is unacceptable as it is unreadable on any other equipment. Discs should be labeled with the book title, computer program used and the chapters included on that disc.

In preparing a manuscript for submission on disc, DO NOT attempt to make it an approximate a typeset page. Aside for ensuring legibility, do not be concerned about the appearance of the resulting printout; consistency is of far more importance. Please follow these basic guidelines:

1.          The electronic manuscript should not contain any commands for page or column breaks, running headers or footers, footnoting, text indent, or multi-column text. At best these commands will simply be ignored by the composition software; at worst, someone will have to remove them. After printing the manuscript, remove automatic footers and page numbering before submitting the disc.

2.          Never type in all caps. Words in caps cannot be changed to lowercase without completely retyping them.

3.          If it all possible please avoid using the "insert symbol" function to insert fractions or to add special punctuation, bullets or letter combinations. Type fractions in the traditional one-slash-two style. Special symbols inserted in PC format often do not convert and must be individually replaced.

4.          Never type the letter "el" (l) when you mean the number "one" (1), and do not interchange "zero" (0) and the capital letter "oh" (O). These will certainly appear different in typeset output and must be changed one at a time.

5.          End paragraphs with one carriage return. The code used for paragraph endings should be used whenever you wish to indicate a required line ending in the final output, as, for example, at the end of lines of poetry, tabular lines, and headings.

6.          Set the indent on the first line of each paragraph using the tab key, not the space bar. Never use multiple spaces for horizontal positioning of text.

7.          Do not add extra vertical space; page composition software can be programmed to change the amount of space that will appear around various text elements such as subheads and extracts. Use the printer commands in your word processor to double-space the printout of the manuscript but submit the disc with single line spacing.

8.          Dashes should be typed as two hyphens, with no space before or after.

9.          Always follow a period with one space, not two.

10.          At line endings, do not divide words by hyphenating and do not put a hard return; both will show up in the middle of a paragraph when the book is formatted. If your word processor has automatic hyphenation, turn it off to prepare your electronic manuscript. Also do not justify your text; it should be ragged on the right edge.

11.        All titles and subheads should be flush with the left text margin of your manuscript and separated with a line space above and below.

12.        Use italic or bold codes within the running text only for words that must remain in those formats in the printed book.

# APPENDIX

This AGREEMENT is made this _____,
_____ (the "Agreement") between -
_____ of _____
(the "Publisher") and _____ (the "Author")
c/o _____ (the "Author's
Agent") with respect to _____ currently
referred to as _____ (the "Work").

In consideration of the parties' promises and obligations as set forth
below, the parties agree as follows:

**1.     RIGHTS GRANTED.** The Author hereby grants and
assigns to the Publisher for the full term of copyright, and renewals
or extensions thereof, the sole and exclusive right to: (a) print,
publish, promote, advertise, distribute and sell the Work in the
_____ language and all other
languages throughout _____("Territory"); and (b) to
exercise or authorize the exercise of any of the other rights in any
other form as provided herein.

If the Author is entitled to terminate the grant of any of these rights
under the copyright laws  of the United States or any other
jurisdiction, all other rights transferred or granted hereunder shall
remain unaffected by such termination.

## 11.    DELIVERY OF THE WORK

**2.2     Elements of the Complete Work.** The Work shall consist
of an approximately _____ page manuscript of text. The
Author shall prepare and deliver the Work according to the

following schedule: the manuscript shall be delivered to the Publisher not later than _____, _____ (the "Early Delivery Date"); and the final, completed manuscript, together with any permissions or clearances and other necessary material shall be delivered to the Publisher not later than _____, _____ (the "Final Delivery Date"). Further, if the Publisher deems an afterward, glossary or some other type of backmatter material necessary for publication of the Work, the Author shall prepare and deliver the requested material by a mutually determined date.

**2.2    Acceptable Delivery. (a)** The Author shall deliver the Work and any other materials   or information required by this Agreement. It shall be supplied at the Author's own expense, in form and content satisfactory to the Publisher and in accordance with the Text Submission Requirements, the Guidelines for Electronic Manuscripts, and the Submission Requirements  for Original Illustrated Art, attached hereto and made a part thereof. Any costs incurred by the Publisher as a result of the Author's failure to meet the specified delivery deadlines or to fulfill the submission requirements shall be charged to the Author, excepting those delays caused by Publisher's requested changes.

**(b)** If permission from others is required for publication of any material contained in the Work, text or visual, or if permission is required for exercise of any other right granted under this Agreement (including without limitation the right to promote the Work), the Author shall secure written permission to reproduce the material throughout the territory in all editions and adaptations of the Work, whether published by the Publisher or its licensees. The Author shall secure such permissions at the Author's own expense and shall submit them, satisfactory to the Publisher in form and content, on the Final Delivery Date specified in Paragraph 2.1. The Author shall consult and cooperate with the Publisher in performing the Author's obligations hereunder.

**2.3    Failure to deliver.** If the Author fails to deliver the complete and finished manuscript and any permissions and clearances required by the Final Delivery Date, unless otherwise agreed upon in writing by the Publisher, the Publisher may, in its sole discretion, terminate this Agreement upon written notice to the Author, and upon receipt of such notice the Author  shall repay to the Publisher all amounts which may have been advanced under this Agreement within thirty (30) days of receipt of such notice.

**2.4    Right to edit.** The Publisher reserves the right, subject to consultation with the Author, to edit the Work submitted by the Author and to request substituted or additional materials before publication. If the Author fails to supply any of the materials specified by this Agreement, or if any of the materials supplied by the Author are unacceptable to the Publisher, the Publisher shall have the right to supply such materials and charge the cost therefore to the Author.

**2.5    Unacceptable delivery.** The Publisher will review the Work and shall notify the Author within sixty (60) days following receipt of the Work whether the material is acceptable or in need of revision. If the Publisher concludes that the Work is unacceptable but could be revised to the Publisher's satisfaction in a timely fashion, the Publisher and the Author shall agree upon the appropriate period of time for the revision process. Should the Publisher determine that the Work as delivered cannot be revised to its satisfaction within a reasonable time period, or if the Publisher determines, in its sole discretion, that the revised manuscript is unacceptable, the Publisher may reject the Work. Upon such rejection, the Publisher shall not be obligated to make any further payments hereunder, and the Author shall use best efforts to sell the Work to another publisher and shall repay to the Publisher any and all sums received under this Agreement out of the first proceeds from such other publisher as and when such monies are received. However, if the Work remains unsold twelve (12) months following rejection, the Author shall promptly repay any and all sums received from the Publisher hereunder. Upon the Publisher's receipt of repayment, the Agreement shall be deemed terminated.

**3.      CORRECTIONS. Text Proofs.** The Author shall read, revise, correct, and return all proofs within the reasonable time stipulated by the Publisher. If alterations in the proofs are made at the Author's request (or because of the Author's failure to deliver accurate copy for   the printer) which cost more than ten percent (10%) of the cost of composition, exclusive of the cost of correcting printers' errors, the Author shall be charged for such excess. The Author shall pay any and all such costs when billed by the Publisher.

**4.      PUBLICATION. (a)** The Publisher shall publish or cause publication of the Work in book form, at the Publisher's own expense, within twelve (12) months of the Publisher's acceptance and approval of the complete and finished Work. The Publisher shall not be responsible for delays caused by force majeure or the act or neglect of a supplier, printer or shipper. In no event shall the Publisher be obligated to publish or cause publication of the Work if, in the Publisher's sole opinion, the Work violates the common law or statutory copyright, or the rights of privacy, publicity, or any other right of any third party or contains libelous or unlawful matter.

**(b)** Decisions regarding the title, format, interior design, and cover for the Work, and all other design, production and publishing decisions are within the Publisher's sole discretion. It is specifically understood and agreed that the Publisher shall own and control any and all rights to any design for the Work created or commissioned by the Publisher, and the Author may not duplicate such design without the Publisher's express prior written consent.

**5.      FAILURE TO PUBLISH.** Provided the Author delivers the Work in accordance   with the delivery dates and requirements specified herein, if the Publisher has not published or caused publication of the Work within the time specified, unless publication has been delayed due to circumstances beyond the Publisher's reasonable control, the Author may give the Publisher written notice of the Author's desire to terminate this Agreement, and if the Publisher then fails to publish the Work within six (6) months following receipt of such notice, this Agreement shall terminate, and the Author shall retain any advances previously received under this Agreement in full settlement of all claims against Publisher.

**6.  COPYRIGHT. (a)** The Publisher shall register the copyright in the Work in the United States Copyright Office in the name of _____ and shall ensure that each copy of the Work published by Publisher contains a copyright notice in such names pursuant to the United States Copyright Act and the Universal Copyright Convention, together with such other notices as the Author may request in writing.

**(b)** Upon the Publisher's request, the Author shall execute any such papers and documents which the Publisher may deem advisable to protect, assign, record, renew, or otherwise perfect or enforce the rights in and to the Work granted to the Publisher hereunder.

**7.  ADVANCE.** Subject to terms and conditions of this Agreement, the Publisher shall pay to the Author, as a non-returnable advance against and on account of all monies accruing to the Author under this Agreement, the sum of _____ (US $_____) payable as follows:

$_____ within thirty (30) days following the receipt by Publisher of a fully executed Agreement.

$_____ within thirty (30) days following the Publisher's receipt and acceptance of all material due the Publisher upon the Early Delivery Date.

$_____ within thirty (30) days following the Publisher's receipt and acceptance of all material due the Publisher upon the Final Delivery Date.

$_____ within thirty (30) days following the Publisher's first publication of the Work.

8.      **ROYALTIES.** Royalties on the Publisher's editions of the Work shall be based upon the net retail sales, less a reasonable reserve for returnable copies, and paid at the following rates:

**(g)**      On copies of a hardcover edition sold in the United States, except as described in subparagraphs (d) through (f) below:

_____% of the suggested retail price on the first _____ copies sold;
_____% of the suggested retail price on the next _____ copies sold;
_____% of the suggested retail price on the next _____ copies sold;
_____% of the suggested retail price on the next _____ copies sold; and
_____% of the suggested retail price on all copies sold thereafter.

**(h)**      On copies of a paperback edition sold in the United States, except as described in subparagraphs (d) through (f) below:

_____% of the suggested retail price on all copies sold.

**(i)** On copies of a board back edition sold in the United States, except as described in subparagraphs (d) through (f) below:

_____% of the suggested retail price on all copies sold.

**(j)** On all copies sold: at a discount of 51% or higher, for special or premium use sales; for export or sale outside the United States; or as a result of the Publisher's mail-order efforts, through couponed advertising, or circulation direct to the customer: 10% of the net amounts received by the Publisher.

**(k)** On copies of any edition sold by the Publisher from any reprinting of _____ thousand (___) copies or less made at least one (1) year after the date of initial publication of the Work: one-half (1/2) of prevailing U.S. rate for that edition based upon cover price.

**(l)** No royalties shall be payable on copies or adaptations of the Work or on ancillary products which are distributed for purposes of promotion or advertising; on copies sold below the Publisher's cost; on portions of the Work sublicensed for publicity use without compensation; or on copies provided to the Author free of charge.

**9.** **SUBSIDIARY RIGHTS. (a)** Pursuant to Paragraph 1, the Author's grant to the Publisher includes the sole and exclusive right to sell or license the Work for use as follows in any language throughout the world upon such terms as the Publisher deems advisable. Except as otherwise specified, the net proceeds of such sales or licenses shall be divided between the Author and the Publisher as follows:

|  | Publisher's Share | Author's Share |
|---|---|---|
| Book club (whether in full length, condensed, or abridged version) | _____% | _____% |
| Foreign publication (which may include the right of such licensee to sublicense certain subsidiary rights in that market) | _____% | _____% |
| Translation (which may include the right of such licensee to sub-license certain subsidiary rights in that market) | _____% | _____% |
| Serial (use of serializations, condensations, excerpts, digests, etc. of text and/or images in news-papers, magazines, other periodicals, books or pamphlets) | _____% | _____% |
| Reprint (whether in full length, condensed, or abridged version) | _____% | _____% |
| Other Book Publication (including, but not limited to, deluxe editions, large print and direct mail editions) | _____% | _____% |
| Storage, retrieval, microfilm, microfiche, other forms of elec-tronic reproduction | _____% | _____% |
| Ancillary Products (i.e. book – or stationary-related product that uses | _____% | _____% |

text and/or images from the Work,
including without limitation books
(e.g. blank or specialty books), stamp
kits, calendars, postboxes, stationery,
bulk notecards and notecard collections,
postcards and postcard collections, day
books, address books, posters, magnets,
gift wrap, photo albums, and photo frames)

Merchandising: including but       _____%      _____%
not limited to the use of title,
text, and/or images to create or
promote commercial products

Performance: TV, radio, sight and    _____%      _____%
sound, and allied rights, visual
reproduction, motion picture,
dramatic and non dramatic

If the Publisher exercises any of the foregoing rights itself instead of licensing others to do so, the royalty rates, where not otherwise specified in Paragraph 8 above, shall be subject to mutual agreement between the parties.

**10.**    **AUTHOR'S COPIES.** The Publisher shall give to the Author, on first publication, _____ (_____) free copies of the hardcover edition of the Work published by the Publisher. The Publisher agrees to ship all such free copies at the Publisher's expense. In addition, the Author shall have the right to purchase copies of the Work at the following discounts for prepaid orders: forty percent (40%) on orders of 1 to 24 copies; fifty percent (50%) on orders of 25 copies or more. All such discounted copies of the Work purchased by the Author shall be shipped at the Author's expense. Copies of the Work provided to the Author under the terms of this Paragraph shall not be resold. All sales of books by the Publisher to the Author are subject to applicable sales tax.

**11.     PUBLICITY. (a)** The Publisher, and any of its licensees or assigns hereunder, shall have the right to use the Author's name, image, likeness, and biography in connection with the exercise of any of such rights, and in advertising and publicity in connection therewith. The Publisher shall provide the Author with an Author Questionnaire, which the Author shall complete and return by a date to be specified by the Publisher. It is understood and agreed that the Author shall provide at the Author's expense a reproducible photograph of the Author that the Publisher may use in connection with the Work and in advertising and promotion of the Work. Any photograph provided by the Author will be deemed approved by the Author. The Author shall cooperate, at the Publisher's expense, in advertising and promotional activities as reasonably requested by the Publisher. The Author shall not compete with the Publisher in promotion and sale of the Work. Notwithstanding anything in the foregoing to the contrary, the Publisher shall obtain the Author's prior written approval before using the Author's name, image, likeness, biography, or the title or any element of the Work in connection with products or services not appropriate for children (e.g. cigarettes, alcohol, condoms, etc.).

**(b)** For publicity or promotion purposes, the Publisher may permit, subject to consultation  with the Author, the broadcast (but not dramatization) by radio or television or on-line, without charge, such selections from the Work as in the opinion of the Publisher may benefit from the sale of the Work. Failure of the Publisher to consult with the Author under this subparagraph 11(b) shall not be deemed a material breach of this Agreement.

**12.     ACCOUNTING AND PAYMENT. (a)** The Publisher shall render semi-annual statements of account to December 31 and June 30 of each year, on or before March 31 and September 30 following, and shall send such statements, together with payment of the amounts due thereon. For each royalty period, the Publisher may withhold a reasonable reserve against returns of books. After two (2) years following the original publication date, if the accumulated earnings from all sources for the Work do not exceed twenty-five dollars ($25), the Publisher may defer a statement and payment until such time as the accumulated earnings for the Work total twenty-five dollars ($25) or more; however, upon the Author's request, the Publisher shall render a statement, regardless of amount due. Should the Author receive an overpayment, it is understood and agreed that the Publisher may deduct such amount from any further earnings of the Work.

**(b)** The Publisher shall pay the Author's share of the proceeds from the sale or license of subsidiary rights as provided in Paragraph 9, less any unearned advances or other debits to the Author's royalty account, within sixty (60) days following the Publisher's receipt of such monies.

**(c )** The Author may, upon written request, examine or cause to be examined through certified public accountants or the Author's qualified representative the Publisher's books of account to the extent that they relate to the sale or licensing of the Work, provided such examinations are limited to one (1) per year and take place during regular business hours. Such examination shall be at the Author's expense; however, if errors of accounting totaling ten percent (10%) or more of the total sums due the Author hereunder are found and agreed to be to the Author's disadvantage, the Publisher shall reimburse the Author for the reasonable out-of-pocket costs of such examination up to the amount of the error.

**13.    AUTHOR'S WARRANTIES. (a)** The Author represents, warrants and covenants that (i) the Author is the sole author of the Work; (ii) the Author is the sole owner of all rights granted hereunder; (iii) the Author has not sold, licensed, assigned, or otherwise encumbered the Work, and will not sell, license, assign, or otherwise encumber, any of such rights; (iv) the Author has the full power to enter into and to perform this Agreement; (v) except for material expressly permitted or cleared pursuant to the provisions of Paragraph 2.2(b), all text, illustrations, and other material contained in the Work is original, previously unpublished, and is not in the public domain, whether as defined under the United States Copyright Act or otherwise; and (vi) the Work in no way violates any copyright or proprietary or contract or personal right of others, including the right of privacy and that it contains nothing unlawful or libelous. The foregoing warranties shall be in effect throughout the term of this Agreement and shall survive its termination.

**(b) Publisher's verification of warranties.** The Publisher shall have no obligation to make an independent investigation to determine whether the foregoing warranties and representations are true, and any such investigation by or for the Publisher shall not constitute a defense to the Author in any action based upon a breach or alleged breach of any of the foregoing representations or warranties of the Author. However, if in the Publisher's reasonable opinion there appears to be a substantial risk of liability to third persons or entities or of governmental action against the Work, the Publisher with the Author's agreement may undertake an investigation, verification and analysis of the Work and implement such revisions of the Work with the approval of the Author which Publisher believes may eliminate or lessen such risk. Notwithstanding anything to the contrary contained herein, in no event shall Publisher be obliged to publish the Work if in its judgment the Work contains libelous material, or its publication would violate the rights of privacy, copyright, or any other rights of any person or entity.

14.      **INDEMNITY. (a)** In the event of any claim, demand, suit, action or proceeding ("Claim") based upon an alleged breach of the Author's warranties, the Publisher shall have      the right to select

counsel to defend itself and the Author, and the Author shall indemnify and hold harmless the Publisher, any seller of the Work, any licensee of a subsidiary right in the Work, and any other person to whom the Publisher or its licensees may extend the representations and warranties contained herein in connection with the production or distribution of the Work or the exercise of any rights therein or derived therefrom, against any losses, damages and expenses (including reasonable legal fees and expenses) arising or resulting from or in connection with any such Claim. The Author shall cooperate fully in the defense of any such Claim, and acknowledges that failure to cooperate in the defense of any Claim shall be deemed a breach of this Agreement. If the Author so chooses, the Author may join in the defense of any Claim with an attorney of the Author's own choosing at the Author's own expense. The Publisher may settle any such Claim against it or waive any appeal of any judgment of a trial court against it. If such Claim is successfully defended or is settled, the Author's indemnity hereunder shall be limited to fifty percent (50%) of the cost of defense and the amount of settlement (if any). Any and all monies awarded to the Publisher in association with a successful defense or settlement shall be shared equally between the Publisher and the Author after the Publisher first recovers its real costs and expenses associated with such defense or settlement.

**(b)** If a Claim is instituted, the party receiving notice of the Claim shall promptly notify the other in writing and shall give the fullest information obtainable at the time of such Claim. Upon receipt of any Claim which would obligate the Author under the above indemnity, the Publisher reserves the right to withhold amounts otherwise payable to the Author and to apply such amounts (as required) in satisfaction of the foregoing indemnities. In addition to any other rights in law and equity, in the event of any material breach by the Author of the Author's warranties, the Publisher may as a final remedy terminate this Agreement and recover any monies advanced to the Author under this Agreement. The foregoing indemnities shall survive the termination of this Agreement.

**15.    DEFENSE OF COPYRIGHT.** In case of any infringement of the copyright of the Work by others, the Publisher may in its discretion sue or employ such remedies as it deems expedient, and all such suits or proceedings shall be at the joint expense of the Author and the Publisher, and the net proceeds of any recovery shall be divided equally between them, but the Author shall not be liable for any expenditure for such purposes in excess of one thousand dollars ($1,000) undertaken by the Publisher without the Author's previous consent in writing, such costs shall be charged to Author's royalty account. If the Author does not consent to all expenditures for such purposes, any recovery shall be divided between the Publisher and the Author in the ratio of their respective expenditures for such purposes. The Author authorizes the Publisher to join as a plaintiff or co-plaintiff in any litigation against one or more third parties for infringement of the copyright in the Work, without cost to the Author, except as provided by this Paragraph.

**16.    COMPETITIVE MATERIAL. (a)** During the term of this Agreement, (i) the Author shall not, without the Publisher's prior written consent, publish or authorize publication by anyone other than the Publisher of any edition or adaptation, abridgment or condensation of the Work or any derivative work (including without limitation, any screenplay, television script, novelization or photonovel); and (ii) the Author will not publish or authorize publication of  any similar material in book, article or pamphlet form, or ancillary product which is likely to directly compete with the sale of the Work.

**(b)** The Author shall not contribute more than 300 words from the Work to any one book, pamphlet or magazine without the Publisher's prior written approval. Further, the Author's name shall not appear on the cover of any other book on the same subject as the Work.

**17.    AUTHOR'S PROPERTY.** The Author shall retain complete copies of all materials provided by the Author to the Publisher for the Work. In the event of loss or damage to the copies delivered to the Publisher, the Publisher's liability shall be limited to the cost of making an additional set of copies if such materials from the set retained by the Author. Except for the loss or damage caused by the Publisher's negligent acts or omissions, the Publisher shall not be responsible for the loss of or damage to any of the Author's property. The Publisher's liability for loss of or damage to any such property shall in no event exceed One Hundred Dollars ($100) for any duplicate slide, Two Hundred Fifty Dollars ($250) for any original transparency or One Thousand Dollars ($1,000) for any original illustration, but in no event shall the Publisher's total liability exceed Ten Thousand Dollars ($10,000). Should the Author require insurance in excess of Ten Thousand Dollars ($10,000), a rider for the excess can be established at the Author's expense.

**18.    OPTION.** The Author shall offer the Publisher the opportunity to acquire the same rights as are herein granted with respect to the Author's next book length work for _____ in the style and substance of the Work, before submitting it to any other publisher whether directly or indirectly. The Publisher shall be entitled to a period of four (4) weeks after submission of such next work within which to notify the Author of Publisher's decision, which period shall in no event commence to run prior to one (1) month after the Publisher's initial publication of the Work hereunder. If within that period the Publisher shall notify the Author of its desire to publish the manuscript, the Publisher shall thereupon negotiate with the Author with respect to the terms of such publication. If the parties are unable to    agree upon the terms within thirty (30) business days after the Author's receipt of the Publisher's offer, the Author shall be free to submit the manuscript elsewhere.

**19.     TERMINATION OF THIS AGREEMENT. (a) Out of print.** If the Work is out of print, and the Publisher does not agree to bring out a new printing or has entered into a sublicense for a reprint edition within six (6) months following receipt of the Author's written notice (unless delayed by circumstances beyond the Publisher's control), this Agreement shall terminate and all rights granted to the Publisher shall revert to the Author upon written request, subject to Publisher's continued participation in any licenses granted by the Publisher.

 **(b) Discontinuance.** If at any time after first publication, the Publisher wishes to discontinue publication for any reason, the Publisher may do so upon written notice to the Author, in which event this Agreement shall terminate and all rights granted hereunder shall revert to the Author upon the termination date set forth in such notice from the Publisher.

**(c) Remainders.** The Publisher may, in its sole discretion, offer copies of the Work for sale as "remainders" at any price it sees fit. The royalty payable upon copies sold as remainders shall be ten (10%) of the amount received, less manufacturing costs, and shall not exceed any other royalty rate set forth in this Agreement. The Publisher shall notify the Author prior to such remaindering and shall offer the Author the opportunity to purchase copies at the estimated remainder price, plus shipping and handling; however, any inadvertent failure to do so shall not be deemed a breach of this Agreement.

**(d) Printer's materials.** For thirty (30) days after the date of such termination, the Author shall have the right, but not the obligation, to purchase any printer's materials under the Publisher's control, at the fair market value thereof. If the Author does not exercise such right within thirty (30) days, the Publisher may dispose of any such materials without further obligation to the Author.

## 20. TERMINATION UNDER U.S. COPYRIGHT LAW.

If, pursuant to the United States Copyright Act, the Author (of, if deceased, the successor of the Author) has the right to terminate the rights granted hereunder, and elects to exercise such rights as provided pursuant to such Act, after such termination, the Author shall not exercise or dispose of such rights except in accordance with the following procedure: commencing with the date of such termination, the Author and the Publisher shall negotiate in good faith for a period of not less than sixty (60) days with respect to mutually agreeable terms and conditions. If the parties are unable in good faith to arrive at a mutually satisfactory agreement for such publication, the Author shall be free to offer the rights terminated elsewhere, provided, however, that prior to entering into any agreement with any such third party, the Author shall first give the Publisher the opportunity to agree, within ten (10) business days, to match the terms offered by such third party which the Author is willing to accept.

## 21. GOVERNING LAW.

Regardless of the place of its actual execution and performance, this Agreement shall be treated as though executed and performed within the State of California, and shall be governed by and interpreted under the laws of the State of California.

## 22. COMPLETE AGREEMENT, MODIFICATION, AND INTERPRETATION.

This Agreement constitutes the complete understanding of the parties, and no waivers or modifications of any provision shall be valid unless in writing, signed by the Author and the Publisher. This Agreement supersedes any prior agreements between the parties with regard to its subject matter, whether oral or written. The waiver of a breach or of a default under any provision hereof shall not be deemed a waiver or any subsequent breach or default. The payment of any advances or royalties hereunder shall not be deemed a waiver by the Publisher of any rights and/or claims that it may have with respect to nonperformance by the Author of the Author's obligations hereunder. The language of this Agreement shall in all cases be construed in accordance with its full and fair meaning.

**23.    ASSIGNMENT.** This Agreement shall be binding upon and shall inure to the benefit of the respective parties, their heirs, executors, administrators, successors and assigns, and may not be assigned by either party without the other's written consent, except that the Publisher may, without the Author's consent, assign this Agreement to its parent, or any subsidiary or affiliated company, or to any company which acquires all or substantially all of its assets.

**24.    NOTICES.** Any and all notices or other communications required or permitted by this Agreement shall be in writing and shall be deemed delivered when personally delivered to the party to whom it is addressed, or in lieu of such personal delivery, five (5) business days after deposit in the United States mail, first class, postage prepaid, addressed to such party at the appropriate address as set forth in this Agreement. Either party may change its address by written notice of such change delivered in accordance with this Paragraph.

IN WITNESS WHEREOF, the parties have duly executed this Agreement the day and year last written below.

AUTHOR                                    NAME OF PUBLISHER


_____          _____

Author's name                             Signature of Publisher


                                                  _____

                                                  Name of Publisher

_____    _____

Date                                    Date

_____

Author's Agent's Tax ID Number

# TEXT SUBMISSION REQUIREMENTS

Form of manuscript. Author shall deliver the manuscript in the English language to _____ ("Publisher") as readable CD-Rom(s) in a word-processing program approved by Publisher, and two (2) complete letter-quality printouts of the entire disc. The manuscript shall be clean and legibly typed and double-spaced with numbered pages. If the manuscript is not in satisfactory form, Publisher may have it retyped and organize it at Author's expense. The accompanying computer disc must follow the guidelines specified below. Author will input all editorial changes onto this disc.

Contents of manuscript. The complete manuscript shall include the following elements: title page; dedication page; preface, foreword, and/or introduction; acknowledgements including credits, if applicable; table of contents; list of illustrations, if applicable; captions, if applicable; text with headings, part titles, and/or chapter titles as needed; an index, if required; and permissions and releases.

Factual Accuracy. The complete manuscript shall be as accurate and factually up-to-date as current information systems allow. For all manuscripts: proper name of people, places, and titles; all statistical and historical information; dates; and permissions must be properly spelled and factually correct. For regional, foreign, and other travel and/or guide books: all of the preceding requirements apply and phone numbers, addresses, directions, fees, and hours of operation must be current and accurate. If the manuscript is deemed factually incorrect at delivery, Publisher may hire fact-checking services at Author's expense.

Quotations and/or sources. All shall be accurate, and the spelling and wording of institutional, corporate, or other proper names shall be correct.

Part titles, chapter titles, and headings. All shall be typed in capital and lower case letters. Part titles should be typed on separate manuscript pages and numbered in sequence with the rest of the text. Headings should be consistent in form throughout the manuscript, though some distinction should be made among different types of headings.

Recipes. Recipes shall be submitted according to the Recipe Guidelines attached.

Bibliography. All entries shall be alphabetized by authors' surnames and form of the information included should be consistent.

Glossary. All entries shall be arranged alphabetically, with the defined term underlined.

Page numbers. All pages shall be numbered.

Photographs, Illustrations, Charts or Graphs. All artwork shall be numbered for identification and, if accompanying specific text, the manuscript must also be cross-referenced to indicate where the appropriate artwork should appear.

Captions. Captions shall be listed separately and each caption identified by the photograph or illustration number it corresponds to. Any credits for photographs or illustrations shall also be typed on a separate page and each credit marked with the corresponding image number.

Author shall also include a letter or memorandum summarizing the contents of the package, noting any offbeat punctuation, unusual spelling, or other areas to which Publisher should pay special attention. See note below about the "insert symbol" function: please call it to our attention when it is used for unusual symbols or spelling in the manuscript.

# GUIDELINES FOR ELECTRONIC MANUSCRIPTS

The manuscript should be submitted on a CD-Rom disc readable by IBM-compatible or Mac computer programs. A manuscript prepared on an electronic typewriter with a disc (a dedicated word processor, such as a Brother, Smith-Corona, etc) is unacceptable as it is unreadable on any other equipment. Discs should be labeled with the book title, computer program used and the chapters included on that disc.

In preparing a manuscript for submission on disc, DO NOT attempt to make it an approximate a typeset page. Aside for ensuring legibility, do not be concerned about the appearance of the resulting printout; consistency is of far more importance. Please follow these basic guidelines:

13.       The electronic manuscript should not contain any commands for page or column breaks, running headers or footers, footnoting, text indent, or multi-column text. At best these commands will simply be ignored by the composition software; at worst, someone will have to remove them. After printing the manuscript, remove automatic footers and page numbering before submitting the disc.

14.       Never type in all caps. Words in caps cannot be changed to lowercase without completely retyping them.

15.       If it all possible please avoid using the "insert symbol" function to insert fractions or to add special punctuation, bullets or letter combinations. Type fractions in the traditional one-slash-two style. Special symbols inserted in PC format often do not convert and must be individually replaced.

16.        Never type the letter "el" (l) when you mean the number "one" (1), and do not interchange "zero" (0) and the capital letter "oh" (O). These will certainly appear different in typeset output and must be changed one at a time.

17.        End paragraphs with one carriage return. The code used for paragraph endings should be used whenever you wish to indicate a required line ending in the final output, as, for example, at the end of lines of poetry, tabular lines, and headings.

18.        Set the indent on the first line of each paragraph using the tab key, not the space bar. Never use multiple spaces for horizontal positioning of text.

19.        Do not add extra vertical space; page composition software can be programmed to change the amount of space that will appear around various text elements such as subheads and extracts. Use the printer commands in your word processor to double-space the printout of the manuscript but submit the disc with single line spacing.

20.        Dashes should be typed as two hyphens, with no space before or after.

21.        Always follow a period with one space, not two.

22.        At line endings, do not divide words by hyphenating and do not put a hard return; both will show up in the middle of a paragraph when the book is formatted. If your word processor has automatic hyphenation, turn it off to prepare your electronic manuscript. Also do not justify your text; it should be ragged on the right edge.

23.          All titles and subheads should be flush with the left text margin of your manuscript and separated with a line space above and below.

24.          Use italic or bold codes within the running text only for words that must remain in those formats in the printed book.

# ABOUT THE AUTHOR

Jim Strader, *CEO & Co-Founder, Quattro Media,* is a 20+ year veteran of the entertainment industry. He has been involved in the entertainment industry as a promoter, creator, writer, producer, manager and publisher. Whether advising in the sale of rights or representing key talent, Strader has been involved in several hundred television shows and movies including *Celebrity Deathmatch, Jimmy Neutron, Santa vs the Snowman, Men in Black, the Matrix, X2, Hellboy, Superman Returns, 30 Days of Night* and *Wanted* among numerous others. He has been at the forefront of deal making for emerging new media platforms since the early 1990's, including internet and mobile content distribution. In 2000, Strader was the only non-attorney invited as a panelist to the American Bar Association's Annual Meeting of the Entertainment Section in Orlando, Florida.

Strader resides in Santa Monica, California with his wife and their two children.

www.ingramcontent.com/pod-product-compliance
Lightning Source LLC
Chambersburg PA
CBHW022127280326
41933CB00007B/578